Somewhere We'll Leave the World

Made in Michigan Writers Series

General Editors
Michael Delp, Interlochen Center for the Arts
M. L. Liebler, Wayne State University

Advisory Editors
Melba Joyce Boyd
Wayne State University

Stuart Dybek
Western Michigan University

Kathleen Glynn

Jerry Herron
Wayne State University

Laura Kasischke
University of Michigan

Thomas Lynch

Frank Rashid
Marygrove College

Doug Stanton

Keith Taylor
University of Michigan

*A complete listing of the books in this series can be found online
at wsupress.wayne.edu*

Somewhere We'll Leave the World

Poems by Russell Thorburn

Wayne State University Press

Detroit

ISBN 978-0-8143-4254-1 (paperback)
ISBN 978-0-8143-4253-4 (e-book)

Library of Congress Control Number: 2017939701

Publication of this book was made possible by a generous gift from The Meijer Foundation.

Wayne State University Press
Leonard N. Simons Building
4809 Woodward Avenue
Detroit, Michigan 48201-1309

Visit us online at wsupress.wayne.edu

For my good friends Jonathan Johnson and Peter Markus—

and those others met in my wandering days
as a young poet, from Michigan to California—

And for my parents, may they forgive me for those days

somewhere
we'll leave the world weighing
no more than when we came,
and the answer will be
the same, your hand in mine,
mine in yours

—Philip Levine

CONTENTS

I

Tracking the Wolf

Winter is a fist, its knuckles bared for blood
and bone of any pugilist who defends himself,
like the bearded hunter with goggled eyes,
who walks the wilderness where men
lose themselves in the snow, struck again
and again by those deft fists—breathless,
eyes swollen from the cold, often doubled
over from the icy gusts. Every whisper fogs
up his glasses; the words he chooses
curse this day of hunting for a wolf.
The rocks he clambered up for a view
slippery underfoot, and the wind threads
its needles through skin. Let the wolf
live, his heart says, but he brought his rifle;
its heft helps him on the snowy path.
For no reason except he's tired, the hunter
settles on a rock to stare up at the moon.
The wolf he's tracked crouches
in the clearing, daring him to shoot,
its frosty fur raised in a kind of whisper,
as the hunter scratches awake a match
to light a cigarette, then pockets its head.
We are all animals, he breathes out in smoke
before the wolf becomes invisible in snow.

The Butcher

Somewhere inside him there's more than his grimy smock
and ten-hour shifts. He dreams of the fox
nosing around the store he wants to escape.
Many days the butcher has felt his worthlessness.
But inhaling a cigarette and blowing it through his soul,
he imagines the heart of a fox, not as meat, but something tender.
The hamburger in his case reminds him of cows
standing in a pasture, as if they could live for another day,
and he hears crows who assault the fox in the open.
All his employees know him only by the name they call him:
Butcher. He begs the fox in its royal fur to take him.
But those animal eyes stare through the pudgy chain-smoker.
His wife drove to Cleveland and never came back; his children
check for his obituary, never return his late-night litany
spoken on answering machines. They know he's reliable
as winter and will never speak any kind words.
Call these dream-aches, the heart from smoking,
like a transistor radio not always able to pick up the right
stations. And he suffers, wide-eyed at the fox scudding
past him. He knows the animal will vanish among slow,
meandering traffic. Snow. He checks on his dream; it's gone
from the store. Moon never shines for him anymore,
in spite of the pet-foods girl saying she's done in an hour.
Her gleaming forehead shows unwashed thoughts.
He returns to the vault—that shudder slams him shut.

The *TV Guide* as the Book of Job

Frozen in his low upholstered chair,
he watches the TV screen
as if he knows angels on the roof
huddle and twist the television tree,
so his own Job figure sees the afternoon
movie all jumbled up, a starlet's
blonde hair bleached from so much static
it leaves her bald. Viewing time
is a stoning, he thinks, dropping his potato
chip bowl onto his lap, and reads
his *TV Guide* to see what's next,
his eyes straining for the fine print
of a forgotten film of the apocalypse.
He fears his fridge in the other room full
of rotten food. Day and night he sits
there unable to walk from his house,
out of a job, and movie after movie
strings him along in nightmare billboards
of horizontal gone wrong. Then, in a
snowstorm that buries the best of everything,
he groans, his bottom sore from his chair
worn out to the springs; the screen glows
when he shuts off the late news,
a ring of green like an alien invasion
that fades for hours to a natural black.

The River He Swims

Hemingway drinks water with his face down
in the Fox River way up in the Upper Peninsula

where a hawk holds its own for a beat
and his mouth chokes from the cold taste

of brown river, frothing salt white round
bent branches in the current like a woman's

spread legs and the open sky visible through
the charcoal oaks ready to harvest leaves

in every color when he returns to his
kneeling position and remembers a woman.

That long walk from the Seney train
gave him thirst and he considers stripping

his clothes to swim through the shoulders
of this river. Every bend of her was sexual.

His belly, that clock, keeps good time
as he rises to his feet and lets the long parade

of fingers begin down his shirt's buttons,
his trousers, and his boots tossed off

and forgotten, he sluices off his underwear
to stand naked for the river—he shudders

about to say her name, and her features
strongly bite him from long ago like flies,

her blonde hair and Polish face,
the mouth suddenly exposed like skin.

Splash, and she's gone, and he barrels on
otter-like for another beat, the stream colder,

and underwater for a moment he wonders
if he will ever love a woman as he does this river.

Many Miles from Home

The dead wood thumped-stacked
when Billy Hall was alive and a star
named after him flickered in a dead bright sky.

Billy said, "Load a cord, Lynchie,
my neighbor won't mind." And piece after piece
filled Billy's truck until you knew

one day he would peer down at you from above.
His house was anywhere his voice cut the cold,
"Keep it moving, Lynchie."

You finally stood there, wood in your hand,
when a squad car rolled up and blinked
its strange, forlorn hello.

You knew Billy could be deported,
looking up at a mizzle of a sky without any purpose.
And a star somewhere twinkled.

His Dublin voice dropped
into a cold marble bowl of thought,
and he stepped closer, shouted,

"You're on your own," and bolted.
You ran down to the beach,
your heartbeat rushing into your navel

when the hound pinched your ankle in its mouth.
The moon watched.
You wanted to know why people died

and women threw back their love
as casually as keys. You fell on your chest,
beat noiselessly every grain of sand,

and the fog cleared away to show you
each star with a name on it and there was yours.
This was what you wanted to tell someone,

but only the stars looked down.
Billy next day said, "Where the hell
have you been?" And you wiped sand

from the stars in your hair, remembering
everything about the night
when fog hungered for clarity and a cord

of wood lay stacked,
winking at you in that relaxed way
wood does before it's burnt.

Union Soldier, after Abandoning His Battle, Forgets Everything Wading through the Shallows

Bone, he thinks, clean right down to bone.
That hole in him where he saw bone,
then blood excused itself for being so bloody.
And he fell naturally in a cornfield, where the ears
heard a musket ball introduce the idea
he might die today.
                              And he remembers
he's thirty years old and unmarried,
and says his name to an audience of flies,
not believing it's his own: to wade through
this brushwork of weeds must be heaven,
except for biting mosquitoes, which he discourages
with a lit cigarette.
                              Barefoot, he squishes
mud up from umber shallows: the debris
of a natural place combing through that disorder
he brought with him, the water soothing
to any other wounds he has forgotten
or dared crump down as his eye catches
a dragonfly in the air, its greenish cylinder
built for unusual flight hanging above
the bog, where this stranger doffs
a sweat-ridden Union cap in midsmoke
and exhales fluff, enough to keep up
with the nearby cigar-shaped cattails.

Ovation: Apollinaire, His Arm a Tremor at the Blackboard

menaced by an eraser, chalk in a drifting
cloud, recalls torn bodies as he lights
the chalk in his mouth, this thought veering

crazy like fifty corpses rising from seats to applaud
the poem the teacher has obliterated: future filled
with airplanes struggling for sky, carefree clouds,

shrapnel so much punctuation. What he can't see
is their desire to become the poem itself,
live this absence, part of the blackboard not

properly erased, his cigarette writing in the air.
Miss Kozlowski, the teacher, stares at him. Her red hair
tied back. Her Polish voice suddenly a sparrow

let in the window unable to escape his sad eyes
of Montmartre, her hands waving at errant hair
addressing her nape. And she sees the children

at this Detroit elementary stand solemn as love,
her smile an easy rhyme. Apollinaire bows, their visitor,
as if all this could vanish before he straightens,

his formidable scar like a signature, that chalk
able to conjure fields of the dead, the earth
this grimace of stubble and cheek, his broad

shoulders rounded in thanks, his breath without shape.
And the teacher brushes dust from her breast,
gestures to the children to sit down.

Bad Men and Dirt

Billy the Kid knew how to run from the law
ride bareback out of Lincoln County
as a ghost in the morning air
a left-handed gun in the mirror
of a fading photograph
an unadorned sombrero and red bandana

And I was him every Saturday
one of the Regulators riding with our ears
tuned to the sounds our mouths made
firing six-shooters in the dark ravine
and a bandana tied loosely around my neck
as if I knew I'd be growing more that day
in the same blue jeans as yesterday

Billy the Kid was a son to an English rancher
who rode nine horses across his ranch
taught Billy how to be a man till
Sheriff Brady led his men in a bushwhacking
Tunstall's dead horse's head laid on his hat's pillow
that day the Lincoln County War
turned Billy into an outlaw

And I always felt left-handed
waging a war that could never be won
looking into a mirror just like Billy
who marauded in backyards
with his own bad men and dirt
walking home after crossing the river
after firing six-shooters with my mouth

The dirt on my knees from crawling
to charge through backyards
in our childhood war
that later became helicopters on television
while my outlaw heart
stayed good for years to come.

Scars

I want to tell you about my scars,
starting with my head crashing
through the windshield.
I want to go back through
the black threads that defined me
on the rainy day of the accident.
My friend Peter lost control of his Beetle.
The man we hit ushered me into his vehicle,
my head of massive bleeding;
I thought he told me not to bloody his seat.
My forehead was stitched, but I never saw battle.
Scars lie, like the mirror when I look
into my eyes and see others
from loving a woman long ago
and not having her child.
I am Frankenstein's monster.
The doctor carved into me;
blood dripped from my lobe.
My nurse, a Native American, made
me laugh, those stitches a signature
waving hairy letters for weeks afterward.
I don't mind scars. The body is eaten
away by its own appetite, darkness
in your eyes stares back, after surgery
my belly pulled inside out like a tire:
scars, all that remain of my childhood.

Sunday Jazz

Breath from nowhere but the body
crouching inside its burden of place,
while the notes one after another blow
from the saxophone as I step out
of my underwear to meet my middle-aged self,
ponder the chest of white hair when once
it was so brown, stand inside the swirling
notes from Coltrane again, in spite of black balls
swollen after surgery, hernia repair through
my belly button. I hesitate before the mirror—
the balls swollen as if there were no hope of love—
one more record to play for the night,
the pain emerging from unexpected
places, like the turntable spinning a record
and those black lungs blowing out the way
we watch ourselves in the mirror, expecting
a stranger to appear. But the mirror is not
the truth, and the body showing gray hair
not a liar. Coltrane describes a moment
with such perfect breath, knowing there is no
answer but his golden bell full of song.
He's not on vinyl but comes from late-night
radio thirty years ago, a friend of mine
in the middle of a late-night show.
And there's Coltrane from Stockholm,
he says, and it's hard to believe Rob fills
the room with his breath. Now he plays
Fathead Newman. I gave you plenty of head
tonight, he says, from a show of Sunday jazz,
with Bill Evans on piano. I heard Rob killed
himself in Brooklyn, had a blonde Muslim
girlfriend, after he left us here in the north country.
But suicide sings sweetly the same old song,
with or without a jazz band. I swallowed pills
once to sleep forever. Breathe, a voice
told me at the hospital. And I listened,
finding that breath was down deep in my belly
and out it came. I was nineteen.

Sergeant Reese Embraces the Suicide Bomber

Reese in full dirty patrol jacket and goggled
        hugs his killer, a boy wired with explosives
at the Internet café in Baghdad,
            bends his mouth to explode this kiss:
"You don't have enough explosives to tame me,"
        and the boy starts to pull away when he feels a stranger's lips

on his cheek, as if betrayal were chrysanthemums
        or a cup of coffee, a crowded café where an eighteen-year-old
woman's smile falls apart like a badly made toy,
          her hair the color of a bleeding frown, a sudden drop
in the temperature when sugar spills fears and chairs
        scatter prayers, rage stripped to lunch.

Those in the blast zone not believing this could be the day.
        The woman in the hijab talking to the soldier
about Hollywood only a moment ago.
          Sergeant Reese, like Steve McQueen, his lieutenant
told him, mad blue eyes, built low down like a wrestler,
        always waiting to run from the law.

But the only law here is irony, what shouldn't go right
        leaves them untouched, a boy who doesn't drink coffee
yet startled to hear Reese from California
          singing Bob Dylan, "not dark yet but it's getting there,"
that five-day-old beard which froze the suicide bomber
        into forgetting why he has come into the crowd:

their café voices silent enough to hear fear exploding.
        Sergeant Reese, who would never rise above the rank
until he beat the burly lieutenant's man
          in the boxing ring at the base—he boxed at home—
breaking free from the boy and posing,
        his fists up, shouting, "Come on, show me what you got."

His father hated seeing him in the ring,

        avoided it at all costs, watching his boy battered

by a big black boxer named Sugar Baby.

                The broken nose and streaming blood, punched

silly, but his mother loved it, came on her own,

        wearing a yellow dress, her mouth rouged up,

ready for her own sexual combat with a man.

        Cheering her baby son on—"Kill the bastard!"—

and good as Reese was he never could.

            He hoped instead for the soft spot of a Hollywood

ending, no harm, that never comes in Iraq.

        And he wants it to come now. Their lives depend

on it, he thinks, a camera shoved at him

        in a close-up for a memory of who we were

through children playing in a disheveled street,

            unable to fully dress itself with missing windows

and so many doors blown off. Even the roofs

        have blown their tops. With chipped cups

bearing an elusive taste of coffee brought up to lips

        unsure if their breath will become a small dust.

Someone like Clive Owen running through the carnage,

           holding onto the only child left in the world.

And Alfonso Cuarón could have caught his heart-

        stopper of a weapon on a table, his fishbowl

helmet off, and that conversation with the woman,

        a shapely form under that tent she hides beneath,

her holes that place he wants to travel,

           if only for ten minutes in the back room. For love.

That's if anyone lives here, if the explosives don't

        blow to hell everything close to love after all.

Sergeant Reese's Letter to a Father

October 9, 2010

I read your letters to crows that flap
overhead, Mesopotamia and more,
but a soldier doesn't care how ancient
a stone is—it's a stone. I love your drawings
of me, if only to remember what glasses
I wore when I was fourteen. I don't remember
much about life with you after the divorce;
your studio up on that California hill
became a shelter for young women,
a free bed in exchange for drawing them nude.
The officer with his cigar growls for us
to climb back inside our overheated Humvee.
Every mile of road caught in our bouncing talk,
the desert moon this evening so white
and inviting like one of your model's asses,
your words chattering crows on the page.
Father, your wish for a happy birthday was shared
with John Lennon, who would have been seventy
if he hadn't been shot in the chest. The shadows
from some Hollywood thriller clutch our hearts.
I fold your letter for my pocket, snake
another line or two before my helmet, a refrigerator
keeping in the heat explodes my head,
and the unspeakable strangeness of being here
at all rubs my soul the wrong way, which
you say is a philosophical orange.

Reese's Letter to a Son

December 8, 2010

Your letter told how Mesopotamian crows
collected on those bodies in the road, and you knew
all their names, you spoke of them as if brothers.
How they died in a Humvee. Now your dog tags,
even buttons off your coat, lie here in this cemetery
of things. Her farm dress buttons, too. Blue buttons
gathered from my mother's dress. The smell of the fabric
returns, other parts of our life erased, but her pockets
torn at the corners bulge again with a gardener's shears,
tomatoes, snap-off beans, a spoon. As a child
I saw her sad eyes full of him, his uniform taken out
to the barn, where he parked his roadster during the war,
and I crawled into the front seat, in and out under
the heavy tarpaulin. Crows flew brainy and tough
throughout the barn, and I squawked back at them
in their own indecent language. In my notebook,
a pencil wielded like a gun, I fought for my father,
but he always remained this erasure, rubber shavings
blown from the heavy page. A shadow of him left,
like his roadster a Ford that never moved, tires gone
and up on blocks, and after my father died
never driven again. Its engine a black sorrow
like the crows who flew through the barn, an engine of stillness
except in my dreams, shifting through all those gears
to grind uphill, imagining my father on the road,
walking slowly behind me in the dust. Your coupe,
son, sits in my Oakland driveway, the dice hanging
from the mirror. When I drive it to the grocery
downhill in rain, I stare into the rearview,
hoping to catch a glimpse of you. Your last letter
from Iraq hangs on my wall with other pages of your face,
helmet on, eyes frightened in a way only someone
like Diego Rivera could consider in his murals.
An ordinary day drifts by and I sit in my chair
a part of all the machinery of death. These drawings
don't match the great Mexican muralist's work,

but as it rains in California, the clouds these huge
erasures of the blue sky, I loop and circle, dot
your eyes looking out from under your helmet,
hoping to remember some part of you already lost.

Sergeant Reese Loves to Box Away His Pain

His father told him he couldn't watch
his son blinded by so many blows
on home leave from not being killed over
in that sandbox of a country.
But his son's the one in the ring right now,
the Saturday night round of pugilists
who love to box away their pain, not the father
who never loved him, or that woman
whose kisses were good as blows to the mouth.
His eyes gouged to slits, as if seeing
through his dreams his mother who kissed
a stranger at the five and dime—her bra clasp
left to unsnap before she slept nude with her son—
and that son's in the ring now, no longer thirteen,
dropping to his knees, breath seeping
from his broken ribs, a glance to the seats
and a glimpse through the cigarette mist
for her, in her middle age and beauty
painted on sparingly. But if we loved our parents,
we wouldn't kill them, the son mumbles,
swallowing some teeth, and he's no longer fifteen,
when he swung at Charley, his best friend,
for telling him his mother's a whore.
Sugar Baby, who hates to hear anything
written within reach of his hook, edits with two jabs,
drops the soldier to the mat, butcher above
a slab of meat. Reese sees not ten fingers
in the referee's hands but twenty, in some kind
of Disney phantasmagoria, but the dancing
black boxer with his sirloin gloves
shouts from somewhere he's king, but he's king
of nothing here; and that soldier boy's
on one knee again, unsure of what he sees,
if he isn't dreaming his mother's in the first row,
wearing a dress low cut and spattered
with his blood and Sugar Baby's, who stands
around him, a man as big as death. And Reese's mother,
in her bosomy dress, first row, seat sixteen,
lipstick like a signpost, whispers yes.

II

Garage Band

Tonight in my garage we're separated by junk,
like a stack of boards my father couldn't throw away.
The rakes and shovels up on the walls, tools
from the old farmer whose house my father bought,
and the three of us lay down our song,
not noticing it's past midnight already.
We walked the piano into the garage last week,
an upright that belonged to my grandmother.
Then John brought his Leslie cabinet so his electric guitar
could go keening through broken panes
in its vibrato. Chris, bent over his Les Paul bass, nodded
his head to the notes unraveling their knots.
We're separated by the engine of my father's
Triumph station wagon that never dropped back into place—
and the work bench behind us threatens with claw hammers,
vise grips from a long time ago. Each of these things
doesn't prevent us from tipping over flower pots
with our sound, waking the neighbors across the
yard in angry lights. Once my mother crept down
the driveway in her curlers to tell us to stop;
a raccoon in his waddle surprised us by stepping
from the rafters and parading across the piano.
John sometimes chases Gary Brooker's vocals
on "A Whiter Shade of Pale." We consider him
our singer because he's the only one who can hold
the right note in his throat before it spills out.
These days have no direction, like the disarray
my father inherited from a farmer, and a klaxon
we crank to announce an air raid that never comes.
We never hear piano chords collapse in silence,
until my mother appears in the doorway.
We pack up for the moon to wail on somehow.
For those draft notices to show up in the mail.
That last whispered guitar break spoken through the air
like someone praying.

Lately My Resemblance to Captain Beefheart Has Been Disturbing

I only saw him once up on stage in Detroit,
where he stepped from his own shadow as Beefheart.
A hand lifted no higher than his eyes, as if he were releasing
dust from the desert, signing to the aliens in the dark
who spoke his strange language of music. I had come
to hear the Kinks, whose drum kit would crumble
during "All Day and All of the Night,"
but there I was suddenly eye-synced with the one
and only Captain. He wasn't in rock clothes
(not like the drunken Ray Davies, whom I adored and would sing
"Waterloo Sunset" as if nothing else in the world mattered),
but in khaki trousers and an oversized shirt,
more for a weekend of urban camping in Detroit
than playing the Eastown Theatre. His eyes of a fish
drowning, perhaps in this river of noise and pollution,
beheld us, his audience. He was the opening act,
and this was around the time of *Trout Mask Replica*,
when Frank Zappa had made his old LA schoolmate
famous after burning his songs in the recording studio.
But the Captain disappeared into a badly tuned misfortune,
a drunken guitar, cigarettes not smoked in time for his muse
to learn. And years later, with my shadow retreating on a stage
that is only metaphor, I wait for the band to start playing behind me.
But there's only a telltale silence, nothing like the buzzing
of amplifiers, and the player piano that was my grandmother's
has long since sunk into waters of forgetfulness.
Late at night, when my family's asleep and my dreams are up
walking around, I watch a middle-aged Beefheart on Letterman
talking about drowning in a sound that he left in paint
for his loneliness, as if he could capture applause in the blowing sand
of the Mojave Desert, where once I walked, keeping pace
with my shadow in a hundred degrees at high noon.

Detroit, on the Bus Headed Downtown, the Driver Is Listening to Chopin's Preludes

for Philip Levine

And why the hell not as he glides past monstrous
rust animals that never quite went extinct,
yearns for a cigarette that he gave up

months ago but not quite a year yet,
as his large hands swerve the bus over
into the faster lane, for the late afternoon

traffic needs to be instructed in good music
as he taps his fingers on the steering wheel,
mouthing the name of Chopin's mother,

Justyna Krzyżanowska, just for its sound.
Now he gains ground on his dreams,
driving up and down the austere avenue,

the preludes under a minute most of the time,
a shiver down his spine as he loses the sure
margin of eternity in the buried white lines,

like a snowy ambuscade he thinks.
His foot jockeys into the next flurry,
a quiet he can't understand, and the blade

of a snowplow grinds metal past him,
as he says over to himself, "Nothing they forged
outlived the rusted gears," before inertia sets

in again and he imagines he's driving a piano
and not a bus down the road he barely sees
through his bright ice-veined windshield.

Without Work

Work is overrated and for those in love
with the sound of the time clock. The coffee break,
the ringing phone, the unexplained occurrence
of the secretary talking to you. When you don't
own a job, it owns you. Your pockets
turn out and your collar pulls up, hair
grows longer, your silences pass without hardship.
Napoleon becomes only an emperor in exile—
your happiness is the sound of leaves blowing
down the boulevard where you don't travel.
A Henry Miller book becomes more than a "geometrical
stiffness" or "a setting in which to place the horse,"
as if you suddenly understood "the horse's ass"
in his painting, as well as "gods and goddesses, devils, bats,
sewing machines, flowerpots, rivers, bridges, locks
and keys, epileptics, coffins, skeletons."
And you are walking out of your own poem to laugh
at all those working this instant, this goddamn second
that splits time like a work whistle. You are tired
of clean clothes, the coffee that keeps you nailed
in your coffin, and imagine a garter, a black mask,
pins, locks of hair—fair hair, dark hair—some
of which catch in the hinge of a little box
and break when a woman opens it. You read Phil Levine's
poem about his mother coming to America on *The Mercy*.
He mentions Pennsylvania, making you think
of your own mother, two years old and at her mother's side,
clutching her flannel nightgown, awakened by the wind,
their Czechoslovakian faces keening on some point
in the wet leaves of the maple trees on the hill
behind their house. Her mother whispers German
to the naked night, beautiful music that her child
will remember and that implodes in your soul
while you stare at wet leaves on a cold early morning,
haunted by all their faces, your father dying of cancer,
wondering when you will work again.

The Chinese Restaurant

Around midnight there is almost no air
left in the snowy landscape. Everything's frozen
and his tail lifts up as his nose goes down,
searching for a trace of a meal. But the fox,
like many of us, remains hungry for food,
and the wisps of ice threaten from the sides
of buildings downtown. The only lights
burning are the Chinese restaurant; he rushes
in when one of the last customers staggers
into the cold and disappears. The fox
doesn't need to check his coat, but a blonde girl
asks him politely. He'd like to lure her
to his den, eat every bit of her lovely arms.
She tells the animal he can eat only what's
on the carryout menu: egg rolls, noodles.
She shows him a table in the corner, not
understanding why a fox would want Chinese
at this hour. Her hips cling to her skirt
as she walks away. The fox in his chair
looks ridiculous. He can't sit there without
his tail making him teeter, and the waitress returns
with his water, her mascara-smeared eyes,
and cheap lipstick. She smiles like neon in need
of a few new tubes to make sense of a burnt-out sign.
The snowplow scrapes the bone of the road;
whatever meat there was earlier tonight
glistens down to icy marrow. A car burns
out its gears trying to move on a mirror.
And the fox, after all an animal, wants
to rip through that skirt: in quick bites
he could have everything. Still, the waitress
hangs there, her pen like a knife wanting
to kill his presence in a few complete sweeps
of her wrist. Even if it says egg rolls to go.
And she knows where they are kept warm
in the kitchen. But there's a slowness
in her hands, a loneliness in her voice
when she asks has he made his decision yet.

Love Allows Us to Walk in the Sweet Music of Our Particular Heart

—Jack Gilbert

We never saw her, the other woman at the museum
who was almost my lover once, in shadow
or around the corner, but watching us admire
Edward Weston's photographs; and she must have
heard us talking about one of his models—his lover
nude on a mountaintop, her nipples in shade.
And I remembered a desire from long ago
and I wonder what her ear heard, like a shell
open to the pitch of an ocean; and I didn't know
I'd hurt her until later. What must she have said
to a friend to justify her departure? To drive the hour
it took for her to get home. Once we kissed
in her kitchen, and with our bodies close
felt a trembling reach our bones. But I was back
at the museum, with someone else from long ago
before all that light and shade, all those peaks
rising up rounded from their mountainous bottoms.
I had loved both women. And I would find out
later that the other had been there, with her blonde hair,
her voice suddenly reduced to a whisper,
trying to make sense of a love long gone.
I didn't suspect there would be a letter.
Or anything from her. But in that urban light
where all was lost, the letter beginning in her mind,
we strode beneath the shadows of large buildings
and continued into the margins at home.

Weekend

My heart was a snow boot stuffed with wool socks,
and the moon in its iced sliver, like a lime
ready for vodka, dared me to drink it down
through the glazier's work in a four-squared glass.
We lay down at the cabin next door
to the house in separate bunks, aware of each other's
breathing, something still sexual between us.
I remembered a freckle on her shoulder,
a marker when I roamed her body.
We heard mice dance over the unswept floor.
And I was aware of my love song,
the heart making such a noise, until an uncomfortable
move in her bunk broke those chords while
she escaped her sleep pose with a flop
onto her side. The almost-deserted house
next door was strange; the old man's laundry flapped,
the caretaker to these woods, whose wife had died.
Maybe I was staring at myself through the four panes
when the caretaker strolled by in his long johns,
holding a rat by its whiskers. There was that odd entourage
of ghostly shadows cast by the bare trees.
Those brassieres and garters hard as boards,
hung in moonlight pure as vodka,
where we had already packed down the snow
with our trek across his property.
Love haunted us in these woods,
our voices raised in argument if we were
still a couple. She wanted company,
someone to talk to while snowshoeing
through these strange parts.

Mr. MacLaverty Has a Pit Bull Named Roscoe

who chases the man across the lawn, his gray hair
in wisps beneath his cap and a step or two
slower now in the cold, as he jams a paper
into the slot. Roscoe, blind in one eye, loses sight
of the middle-aged paperboy, who pulls up
the frayed collar of his old coat for the first flakes
of snow and slides across the stone driveway.

He was told the pit bull would lick him to death,
but fear, that other old bone, has been gnawed on
too many times by him, unshaven and weary
of delivering papers with his younger wife.
He wears a fine collar of white; the snow in its
homespun threads weaves everything lace.
He stumbles away from Roscoe, who sometimes
trails him all the way down the hill.

But that bag bouncing off his balls reminds him
of his wife seated in her rusty car; he thinks how
she has tried to bust them each time
by filling that filthy bag with more papers.
Sunday morning in snow, Roscoe at the top
of the hill peers down with one good eye,
deciding if that trespassing shadow deserves licking,
and he starts his slow descent till hands
that reach yank him by his leash.

Across the Street from His House, a Boy, the Oldest of Sixteen, at His Father's Grave

The wind changes voices as he stands
in his father's grave, voice of dark, bitter wind
      taking hold;
Lynch, oldest of sixteen, hoists up the twins,
      his mother's jewels,
and they are kicking and laughing while they peer
      up at a neighbor widow
looking down the end of her Camel cigarette.
She smells of smoke and gin, her feet muddied
      from rain and the wake
still burning in the Lynch house across
      the graveyard,
the phonograph still scratching out Sinatra
as their father listens in his coffin.
And all the sons and daughters rush out of the hole,
      Sunday clothes soiled
as they hear a banshee chasing them. But Lynch,
      the oldest, stops dead
in his tracks when he hears the widow stutter, "Come
      here and give a lady your arm."
He sets down the twins, telling them to scurry back
      through the mud.
He walks the widow home through whiskered grass,
and the moon comes unhinged.
Her lipstick aglow in the mist, she seizes his arm.
      A tongue quickly in his ear tells him love
is weary and always searching for a moan
in the night; his father's voice echoing above
      the bent pine trees, living, laughing,
repentant of all his sins.

Garage Band Records at Magic City

Detroit, 1972

All of us were good Catholic boys who prayed
our lottery number wouldn't come up for the draft.
And when we found the studio wanted to give us
an hour to record free, we hoped our drummer
would be there to steady us on his skins.
Kenny was black. He partied with us in the suburbs
and was a hemophiliac. He liked to ride around
in our singer's Jaguar. Kenny never showed up
with his drums. And we lost our nerve.
John began counting but I couldn't hear him.
My first piano chord crashed late under my fingers,
a desperate noise, something akin to prayer.
His electric guitar played through a Leslie speaker.
I sat at the piano, wanting to take back that chord.
John's guitar through the Leslie sounded like Clapton
on "Presence of the Lord." I remembered
the late-night news and the vinyl of body bags.
And before the song was over, I thought how far
we had come to end up nowhere. At the piano,
leaning into the chords was my way to stay alive.
But we had a bad singer, and I saw the engineer
take John aside and beg him, "Can you return
and redo those vocals?" He fingered a few notes
on his guitar, as if letting it think for him.
His slowness in responding said no, for
without a drummer it wasn't worth it. For hours
we had practiced, those letters from the draft
board maybe in the mail. The suburbs held us in their sway,
and boards in my garage sometimes rattled
when we played louder than normal, as if we could blow
the roof off the garage and find gratitude
in a buzzing amplifier. The studio was where voices
fit the right dreams—and some of them blew out
through the hole in the wall. Others ended up
crumpled paper on the floor. Like songs
that could never be sung. I studied one or two

carefully. We had come to an end somehow.
And I dropped the wrinkled verse to the floor,
prepared for nothing but the next chord, knowing
all the songs I'd ever write would die.

The Mountains Didn't Know I Was Playing a Piano

owned by a convict's mother, a Lowrey spinet
whose minor chords slid off branches
like wet snow. She had died and I played
for his mother. I wanted to get it right.
I sat on the bench as my left hand walked
up the mountainside to this Idaho house.
The convict sold the piano for a song,
and so I paid the difference with these melancholy
chords. We, the three poets, had slept
that night in Jonathan's cabin, and now
Jonathan and I visited his uncle Steve.
The four of us had played poker last night,
and used poker names around the table.
Mine was Hawk. (The Hawk, a very charitable fellow,
when he won yet another hand of matchsticks
and quarters, offered a loan to the losers.)
Shann's was Stang for the Mustang he drove;
Jonathan's was Juice; and I'd already forgotten Steve's.
When I won a large pot with a pair of aces
it made me think of a wife with fingers
of luck pulling in the winnings, her buttocks
of swans' backs—and André Breton's
poem for his wife with hair of wood fire
and teeth the tracks of white mice on white earth
came to me, but I never told anyone.
I didn't want to touch my luck, luck the convict
didn't have for a murder charge against
years of solitude. My left hand was free
at his mother's piano and walked up the mountain;
and the right almost laughed at the unshaven look of us,
free men, as the music filled Steve's kitchen,
the chords obeyed their own kind of luck
to my hands discovering them, and the cold morning
in Idaho sang of sawed wood and the wood fire
of a wife's armpits, that hard luck some men
found before their first coffee.

John Lennon on the Beach in the Upper Peninsula

His hair is still long at seventy, his body's thin
as an addict's, and I'm almost sixty, wondering how
he leaves his skintight black trousers as a pool
where nobody should walk. Cold—everything tingles—and the sun
hides behind sinister clouds. A dream of winter,
the Vikings floating in their open boats.

I see Lennon throw aside his Spaniard hat,
his round mirrored sunglasses he wore when he and Dylan
drove around New York. I want to swim naked
in the water with him, strain my vocal cords like him—the cold's one
way to keep the past alive—his Rickenbacker left on the shore.

I blow on my hands as he enters the frilly foam,
his legs lifted like a crane or old lady, I can't decide which;
and that boy who bought *Rubber Soul* one day in December,
my big plastic glasses sliding down a greasy nose, bangs
reaching my brow, hears him sing "Norwegian Wood,"
what I needled over and over on my scratchy record player,
for the sitar but mostly the bath he slept in at a girlfriend's room.

Just the idea that John's here, his arms wrapped around his body,
like some whaler whose ship went down, glows in me like fire.
When he bathes in the cold, he blubbers a whale's mating call,
or maybe it's only an old man's complaint,
and I turn around to pick up his Rickenbacker—strum
the twelve strings, while John's doing the breaststroke

out to the rock, and I pretend I'm him. I slip the guitar strap
on. As he gasps in the soft white waves that will shrivel his skin,
I build chords till snow falls, guilty of withering
every bare bottom, watering eyes—and as I look
for Lennon in Lake Superior, my fingers ache
from the strings, and I know that boy behind those glasses
was always in pain. And the Vikings rest in their boats,
the oars pulled up.

I stare at them, then the rolling water, currents
undetectable, and Lennon's gone. His nasty sneer
he keeps curled under his lips gone as well.
His bony nose without a septum—gone.
All the people living for today—yeah, gone.
The idea that he was bigger than Christ.

Robbie Robertson Decides to Hitchhike Back to Canada

He walks away from his broken-down truck,
the radio still emptying into the falling snow.
He thinks of notes as bloody as fists
and begins singing to the darkening woods.
His thumb is medieval almost, some tool
that Beowulf would have used, if he could have
hitched a ride with Grendel down to a marshy,
desolate fen, but he's Robbie Robertson,
and he doesn't know much more than
a dumb shit from nowhere. And that's where
he was riding to on a deserted road above Idaho,
road that became bumpier, no guardrails
to protect the wayward from a fatal descent.

"I ain't going far tonight," he growls
to the illuminated eyes in the woods—the wind
in its whipping left him sure he should have brought
a jacket heavier than leather. But he kicks at the road,
and it comes apart, gravel and rock, something
forgotten—and he sings more notes, bigger ones
that could hold a whole band playing.

That's when he confesses to the ghost of Levon
in the ditch: "The tired dressing rooms, broken mirrors
with so many lives just as broken, the arenas, but before
that the jukebox bars, heartache dancing on top
of tables—we traveled together—all of us
and now you have keys for some dream convertible
that never requires gas."

And he pauses here to shiver, then recollect how
Richard Manuel died, hung from a shower
stall after playing a Florida lounge in hell.
But Robbie wasn't there to save his life, and as the moon
in its chrome fender rides through the bruised sky,
he wonders who will save him tonight.

On a Bus Headed East on US 2 in a Late-Night Blizzard Years Ago

Snow with big fists pounds against
the windows and our driver sits
in his filament of a chair. He is a bulb,
burning like one on a porch. His light
touches us on the bus; the burly black man
who resembles Isaac Hayes sings for a woman
he is always leaving and coming home to.
His songs must weary him; he keeps singing
as if it were religion. Many dark thoughts
occupy my time as we approach six a.m.
and the St. Ignace pantry for the poor.
Inside, we will wait for the next bus:
aspirin bottles, some toilet rolls, canned goods
with faded labels up on the shelves.
But we're not there. The bus shudders in the snow,
the falling snow in its own movie shot
by a Swedish director; and I seem to be one
of the characters. The reading light illumines
a page of Richard Brautigan. I remember him
checking in to the hotel where I worked.
He told me his toilet was out of order.
I marched upstairs, flushed it once—in perfect
working condition. On his bed a fifth of vodka
and a *Playboy*. I turn the pages of *Trout Fishing
in America*, thinking about his hotel bed,
his suicide from a shotgun in Montana.
I listen to Isaac Hayes, with his luminous voice,
attract us to his light; his broad shoulders
fill the chair with its huge bones of a man
who won't let us go without a fight.
But the night grows longer and I feel myself
giving in to something I can't name, and shove
my head against the cold window of Lake Michigan,
and watch the whitecaps in the dark, as if the miles
were the only way to kill one's self.

III

Gravitational Field

All the spring peepers back in the swamp
singing, the moon this whole chord
of bone, as if it knows what seventy years

sounds like—and another seven million—
because I don't, as I imagine John Lennon
seventy: hair gray, slouching over his guitar.

Something about the moon tonight
tells me he can wear a sloppy Spaniard's hat
and walk down the grocery aisle

and be anyone he wants, an ex-Beatle
who never died, May Pang beautiful as ever
but fifty, watching him squeeze tomatoes.

His companion all those years who returned
with him to New York, and in the dark
of the upper Midwest, these dreams

reassure me somehow about the good
in the world, me, in my fifties,
wanting that locomotive sound

of his chords, the guitars
chopping sentences into this chill
riding up my spine, and those peepers

like fists clenched won't remain
silent, in their chorus. Rain is coming
but not yet, and if aliens descending

upon New York City were seen
by John and May up on a Fifty-Second Avenue roof,
then that sentimental train

that rocks your life can leave
you staring up at the sky, without a job,
and your pockets full of Lennon

give you an edge in your isolation,
singing loud as you can with the peepers
in their sexual frustration.

There is something grim about a large
moon unburdening itself though,
for the hard truth is simple

to understand: a bullet from an assassin
killed John Lennon, despite the soft shot
Phil Spector emptied into the recording

studio roof—and those vodka-fueled
vocals didn't kill his career, for later,
headphoned and deep into "#9 Dream,"

one of the most beautiful love songs ever made,
May Pang whispering into the microphone "John,"
he might have felt the gravitational field

altering, the earth below his feet shake a little,
for he believed in woman—and would sing that song,
as if believing in aliens, anything

to keep him alive until seventy, for his heart
to cover the moon, and he would have
returned for good to May.

The Blind Guitarist Whose Six Strings Can Only Play Him So Far

He travels with his guitar his fingers up on the neck
for him to see the road he must travel blind

his right hand strumming how he walks that road
his classical guitar autographed by Willie Nelson

who once played in a bar nearby in Juárez
and whispered you play like no other

but left Manuel in the shadows
searching for his song beyond the next fret

like a dry riverbed or moonlight broken
apart with an axe

His wife deserted him in Dallas after he joined
a small bar band and drank his earnings

sometimes alone in a room beneath
the gaze of a stranger he remembers his hand

in her dark Spanish hair—she told him
nothing before she packed her suitcase

leaving him there on the edge of love
his guitar in the corner looking on

Mostly he walks the music he plays
on his autographed guitar a hole in the back

from a bar fight and Willie's moniker
on the cracked pickguard

the notes mishandled when he falls
down an arroyo strangling the neck

with that fear which turned back
an attacker's knife into the man's chest

as if he could never get it right now
rising in slow motion from the rocks

and knowing on top of that ridge
the patrol car was tracking down his dust.

Drawing Elena

My hair grown gray as an oracle's,
I open the sketch pad to draw her nude.
Her black ringlets wet over her ears.
She drains the noodles, a young woman
with a child who lives with his father,
the photo she shows me wrinkled
from a pocket too close to the skin.
I grasp my pencil and look at the pad
as if it were opening a door I could fall through.
Her skin as soft as everything I need to touch
and breathe in: she doesn't mind me looking
at her apple blossom breasts, measuring her navel
as the center of her soul. She sets the table,
pours wine. I promise myself to finish drawing her.
The trees comb their hair with branches,
the darkness around that bone shining dimly
through precipitation. I hear the crickets' holocaust,
the grass tiptoe as the wind blows across its ankles.
A studio in the ancient hills, my eardrums ring
with bells of thunder. Every day I walk the hill
for my mail. I believe there's a way to reach
a soul through rain and light. A fire sings
through her eyes once she removes her glasses,
purrs a tune, then wraps her fork around noodles;
she smiles at my paunch, poses as if her heart
were willing to find a home in me. Lightning zigzags,
darkens, sticks like leaves to the window,
and I bend to her raw places.

Movie House

Did the blonde notice his strides
taking him across the old railroad yard?
He cuts across the field from the gallery,
thinks about erasure in the drawings
as he walks over the overgrown train tracks
and stares up from this dizzy earth at the bugs,
so many he feels like he's in a silent movie;
with his brooding that tears at his chest,
he has broken into the movie house of himself,
his recurring dream of being a drawing
comes alive, his feet trip over loose bricks,
and he remembers the art on pedestals—miles
of foil or string shaped into objects—an egg
carved from wood, a breast's luminescence
smiling with its huge tit. With his camera
concealed in his shirt (a breast or two from
the blonde who wants her nudes back)
he caught others observing art: he will blow
them up in his dark room, admire the grainy skin
horses leap over, the sexuality of color in freckles,
then discourse to the blank television how
an artery in a neck bulges like a fire escape.
He'll scribble titles on these photographs
before he sells them, adds his name,
a severe sinuosity, an obscene waving
as it penetrates the corner, an ambush
like Zorro's letter, except it's an X.
But the nudes of the blonde who wants
them back?—those photos he keeps.

American Killer

Father, I am an American killer
deep in his combat boots and sunglasses,
drinking coffee on patrol and copping a look
at the Muslim woman who hides Flaubert
under a crumpled newspaper at the Internet
café with imported marble tables.
She has long hands that pour out of her
heavy attire, fingers that can pull the pin
of a hand grenade. She reads Bovary's
adultery in Yonville, measuring how far
she can parade without being stoned.
She knows Emma would have been lined up
against a wall and stoned, in this city
where the sound of steps thunder,
or coffee cups rattle before murder.
Father, I am in love with her daring eyes
that stare up from her suicide.
Then I see you working in your studio,
your pencil in judgment suddenly
drawing a female's torso, her curves
asking little of you except truth.
I am for fighting a Hollywood ending
of drone-led erasures on neighborhoods.
But she swirls a fingertip around the edge
of her small cup of espresso at the table
farthest from the door and me, the son
of a drawer in California, in combat boots.
Those women stoned for their ability to read—
I wonder if they'd have chosen Emma Bovary
to die for in a café. She drinks me in finally,
as if seeing a drone that someday would kill
her family, looks deep at my unshaven face,
all that was wrong in a mountain of rubble.

When One Tugs at a Single Thing in Nature, He Finds It Attached to the Rest of the World

And he treks home from his truck
broken down on the road, its plow blade
dropped like a jaw at the bone-breaking cold.
The pickup full of wood not moving,
he'll have to return in the morning
when it's light, but for now he's got John Muir
in his pocket and feels safe with
the aurora borealis in its labor
of green faintly glowing above the screen
of upright trees, which are not going
anywhere either, and remain as a silhouette
with the jack pines. Despite the breakdown,
a song curls his lips into a smile,
something from long ago and the creek breathing
through many cracks makes a silent noise
in reply. He has miles to walk before
he reaches home, no trouble for him.
He's a working man, whistles a tune
that hurts his chapped lips
because of the cold, and his family must realize
he's not on time for supper.
And he stops to look up at the stars,
every one part of a pattern
hard to understand: his feet on the road
down a whole step, scuffing along
like a guitar's loosely played chords,
the heart open for his footsteps.

Hollywood

Love won't hurt anyone.
Those words are only paper, desire
more like the conversation burning
in an angry woman's face, say Marilyn
Monroe screaming at Arthur Miller
for being a murderer. You are killing yourself
with love, your shirt unbuttoned,
hoping you hear a reply from nobody
as you walk around Hollywood,
a rumpled newspaper under your arm,
cigarettes like lies everywhere, the morning
barely begun but hours old for a failed screenplay.
Your passion won't bring you love, and you
peer into the Writers Guild window, wishing
somebody was reading your script. You typed
it on an Olivetti, by God, and sang of Beckett
in America and confronted by Allen Ginsberg
at a New York City café. In another café,
where the brokenhearted have gathered for years,
Chekhov completes his encounters with Buster Keaton,
aged but agile. Love lasts by not lasting.
In Keaton's eyes you can still see the ashes where love
burnt down his wife and mansion with his movie company.
All those good years gone, and the arches of your
feet are sore and like the voices of children, according
to Jack Gilbert, poet of many fires now dead.
Down in Hollywood, you are a middle-aged poet
and want to pet Monroe's slouching shoulders,
say Arthur is a murderer. Your son drives
around the block, these few minutes for you
without a lifeline, who searched for Jack Nicholson
yesterday in Studio City, hoping he knew why
love never lasts. But his black Mercedes never appeared
and you shared an eight-dollar muffin with your son
at the Aroma Café, where you heard Marilyn
talking at another table, her voice sweet

as that darkness lying over fields in the early evening.
He lets you wander another block, those
lost fires in your burning still for a woman,
fire started from whorls of scrub in the canyon.
Love is eaten by flames, you whisper to your shadow
leading you nowhere but down dirty sidewalk.
On the subway to downtown LA
you watched a transvestite swing her
or his body around a stripper's pole.
She shouted at her audience, Look at me,
but you turned away, as if you were
a disgusted Clark Gable after roping
a mustang on the set of *The Misfits*, knowing
you'd only cut the lariat you used to pull
down a horse for Marilyn, the recently divorced
Roslyn, in Arthur Miller's screenplay.
He was Marilyn's husband until love burnt
them up, and you wait for your son to drive
around the block one more time before you wave
to him you are here, you will never be anybody.

(with lines of Jack Gilbert)

Walt Whitman Wears a Huge Hat in the Noonday Heat

His gray beard collects dust
of the natural world where he pushes
his shopping cart through the desert.
The wheels jam in the sand and rocks,
all his clothes stuffed in black plastic bags,
and he inhales great draughts of space:
I am larger, better than I thought;
I did not know I held so much goodness.
But those words dribble from his beard,
addressing nobody in particular;
he shoves his cart, caught in the sand,
and hears voices, as if walking any aisle
today in Walmart, announce their specials:
those who were slaughtered,
the former wound-dresser can't deny.
His beard never so tangled
with the dreams of others that have
never been realized. Now,
as if a thousand beautiful forms
of men and women have astonished him,
he bows his long-haired head,
that floppy hat brim bent over his brow,
as he stands in this world,
with its emptiness he can't account for,
but must cross before evening.
All seems beautiful to me, he says
hoarsely, suffering from asthma,
so he has to breathe fresh air. Ahead
of him, in the boulders on top
of each other, their surface so smooth
and clean, he sees, lovers alone,
embracing in their stone.

John Huston Talks to Clark Gable about His Next Scene as a Drunk Falling Off a Car Hood

where one can leave himself for dead,
alcohol-lit words asking for trouble,

as he tells his actor to stagger through the bar
under the rack of Fresnel lights and slide

off the hood of a parked car outside
and the sixty-year-old Gable will fall hard

like any cowboy in love with alcohol,
in love with the holes his feet

step drunk, in love with women,
their soft curves a puffy whiteness covering

every bruise of an embrace, in love with all
the wrong words spoken about love.

His son and daughter came to the rodeo
and hearing he was in the bar

waited for him, but the cowboy had
too many bottles by then.

He rises at the table of empties,
Gable playing the father whose eyes

burned like a bull let out
of its pen for the rodeo,

slides off the hood of a car,
where he catches Marilyn watching him.

He remembers his costar at sunset,
her bare nape and white-blonde hair,

her dress with those polka dots,
as she looks away, just looks away.

No bones broken, but his head
in orbit somewhere else, he dusts off his legs,

dizzy from all his bones sensing
they'd never make it home.

Broken

Those electrical lines broken from
the weight of ice, and the TV
stares coldly at the shivering couple,
who complain of their misfortunes
like Job. The water pipes frozen
and the cold so heavy now,
they wear it like coats, wondering
when the thaw will come. Their
last winter storm they called Maximus,
after a Roman general, and the redhead,
lighting a smoke from the gas burner,
tilts her blue eyes up at her bald husband
and says, better if we name blizzards
after actors like Brando who never
remembered lines but always froze
the voice of someone else trying
to ripple muscles in a fight scene.
The truck hasn't started in days:
the apocalypse is here to stay,
says the man in his grisly beard.

Broken in his voice his love
for somewhere warmer, like their bed
where he hasn't satisfied his wife's
chilly desire for days, but how
heat sleeps in dreams, brassieres
with their molded cups of a goddess
left on the floor as his wife dons
flannel and mittens for bed.
He remembers when he watched the moon
shatter from cold as Zhivago
warmed up his pen to break the ice
of poetry, at Varykino, late at night.
Yes, if you name the next storm, it should
be after Brando, winces his wife tightly
wrapped in a Hudson Bay blanket.
But everything's broken, including love,

the sleeping bag falling to the floor,
as he climbs from his couch, as if he were
someone else walking barefoot
to weep at the frozen window, the moon
that hung there in its pale fire
like a place Bolsheviks headed for
on a train that breathed only fire.

Winter Road All Bone, Miles Past Kiva, US 41 Headed North

Through the shadowy grin of six a.m.
       after delivering a son to the airport
and tuning the radio to another station,
           I remember when I swallowed
my mother's pills, unaware they
       were only painkillers and not sleeping pills.
And I survived to feel starched sheets
       of a bed, the finger of a beautiful
doctor named Slaughter up my ass.

My father never got lost
       behind the wheel because he stuck
a suction compass on his dashboard.
         I stare into the night road ahead,
radio turned bone-chilling loud
       to later Dylan who sings about a darkness
not there yet. His voice in its throaty crooning
       almost gone from eighty cigarettes
a day once, and I wonder what it's like
       to chain yourself to so many bad things

in a row, wintry thoughts, bones
       and the ghostly fields when they appear.
Through this early morning burden
        I want my father to tell me
it's all right, the road is dry and straight,
       and you're already nearing Trenary now,
almost home. And I think about my near-death
       and my father carrying my teenage body
out to the car and the hospital

where they would pump my stomach.
       Father, you failed many times,
but I long to share this road with you, a road
        that was never ours.
The cigarettes my mother smoked
       never killed me but it did her in the end,
that slender woman with a starlet's face
       I never revered until she was gone
and her voice crumbled in my head,

a fragile vase, without value,

        smashed apart and not to be replaced

when she heaved her last breath in the hospital,

           where I prayed beside her, with you.

I share this road with both of you, Father.

        The headlights looking, always looking

for something not there, and every hurt

        searches the road for barns

or signs that say not yet but almost home.

IV

Marmalade

What the photographer doesn't know
(and why we are photographed skulking
through the lobby of the hotel
with sleeping bags, a bottle of wine
poking its corked head out of my pack,
unshaven after a night in Idaho
and sleeping at Jonathan's cabin)
is that we are celebrities. Our faces
have stared back at those hungry fingers
clutching our books of poetry,
that hunger for fame in our eyes
captured by a friend or wife
who may not understand why we are
trying to rip through that reality
of words on a page, our appetite
for the grander scale (why we have settled
in comfortable chairs at our table
in the ballroom—chandelier, concierge,
friendly expensive breakfasts—and why not
sip some wine in a coffee cup there).
We'll learn later about our mugs up
on the screen for educational purposes:
see, even celebrities forget to shave
and carry sleeping bags to their table.
The photographer (whom we saw snapping
at the air, and I like to think he's employed
Ezra Pound's aesthetic in deciding
what history to canto-ize) caught us
drinking coffee with a slender waitress
who has a two-year-old daughter,
and it's for her physique and the child
that I'll leave five dollars. The coffee delivers
the mountains again, a catalog of notes
on living with the snowy peaks of Idaho,
where we slept in Jonathan's roughly hewn
cabin with his shelves of poetry books;
and one threaded through my hands

words Kenneth Koch wrote years ago.
We are living the high life, first
the mountains and our reading, then
poker through the night with assumed names.
Mine was Hawk, and with a pair of aces
I beat the other hands to win the matchsticks
and quarters. Now the Davenport Hotel,
clean linen (hand towels in the bathroom),
and my order of white toast, marmalade,
and over-easy eggs, the coffee talking
instead of me about Dr. Sax and the childhood
glimpsed through shadowy pages of Jack Kerouac's
eponymous novel Grove Press printed long
ago. Hallelujah, I am a bum, I think
with fine tastes—an educated wastrel
who sits here in good company. Our waitress
appears at our side as if she has been shaken
out of a magician's handkerchief—presto,
and she's refilling my coffee. Her blonde
hair tightly ponied back somehow, dare
I ask how many hairpins? And so skinny,
as if she has done this magician's trick
too many times to survive. What are the
poets talking about? The chandeliers
must have spy cameras, maybe I am referencing
George Smiley's quiet spydom in *Tinker,*
Tailor, Soldier, Spy—the novel and the current
movie. That photographer with his camera
lingers in the hotel lobby large enough
for a whale, a fishing boat, a lesser-sized
iceberg; and we are talking about the bus
ride back to Cheney, where Jonathan lives
some twenty miles away, the curious head of the wine
bottle listening from my backpack (and bless its
pointed little head), poems that need to bulk
up inside us, while his eyes hold that hull
of a ship going down off Spain's coast,
the edge of emptiness in all those Jack Gilbert
spaces between the words. And I scratch my chin,
wondering if I could strike a match head from that

stubble, munch on more toast with marmalade,
sip coffee dark as those waters where a good
poem goes to die—and sometimes is raised
gleaming in Mediterranean light, with hair
of sea weed combed slick over its skull, the mermaid
on the prow so dangerous with its breasts
for poets with wives to consider. A flashbulb
silently consumes us again, maybe catching me
licking that marmalade spoon, or sitting
suddenly weary and wondering what I miss most
about my middle years with women who
never correspond back or bother to call
(lost like sunken ships off the coast of some
desire with its memorable chests).

Billy the Kid Smells Cinnamon in Texas after a Bad Night

All is clean except our mouths…
—Michael Ondaatje

The porch lights spill
into the desert; cups of coffee
and the smell of cinnamon wake up
William Bonney—like a Gila
monster's tongue, he thinks
at the end of his nose
looking up from a couch where
the torn skirt of Sallie's nightgown
paints dust and cobwebs
are strung and clinging like his outlaw
days—and Pat Garrett asleep
in the rocking chair still,
his killer certainly, but young
Bonney doesn't know that yet.
Whiskey has killed him and the others,
Sallie with her cinnamon hair
of some trade he imagines sexual
bending down to his buck
tooth like a bullet ready to be loaded
into words: *what have you
put into the coffee—
that whiskey can't beat—*
and the moon a woman's
pale breast hangs still
in its noose above the land.

But I don't want to die,
he spits out
from his sip of coffee, like
some exotic place
he can't remember dreaming of.
His English rancher father figure,
John Tunstall, dead in
the Lincoln County War,

and many others dead
but not as dead
as them from whiskey drinking.
Clotheslines like shoulders
pinched high up
in the Texas air with their legs
kicking below the ghostly
shirts brightening
his desire for Angie. Damn
cinnamon, he says,
it smells of your body
and it grows twenty feet
tall from Herodotus,
words Tunstall breathed
through his English speech,
as if he were drunk on
the history of every damn
thing time has grown.

Expecting Someone to Come Walking through the Snow, Say, Jim Harrison

I'm searching for a way to be younger,
like Harrison who wrote of being twenty
in the snow of Leningrad, when he visited Russia
and looked for Yesenin, but in this snow
it's hard to return to one's youth, wade
through the same waist-high drifts.
A noose of branches scrapes together,
crows in their hunger fight for bread ends
thrown from our balcony by my wife.
I didn't expect Harrison to hobble by,
with a bad hip and hating seventy, his hair whiter
than the color of his Indian-esque youth.
Old age is an acquired taste, like selecting
a white Cadillac from a showroom when
the speedometer reads to a hundred and driving
only dream boulevards in the dark.
Those crows surprise me with their agility,
in the thin soup of sky; the wind builds
a cathedral out of the orchard; those waving
branches are the elbows of guitarists hard
at work. I'm learning something from sixty,
in spite of Harrison standing there like
a pale tree, no hat on in the snow,
the crows trying to land on his shoulders.
Let Russia move closer to our backyard.
All those guitarists in the orchard play
at night, slapping chords in a blues song
that nobody but the wind understands.
Yesenin removes the rope from his neck that years
ago killed him. I listen to the storm
in its monotonous music, find women left unloved,
and that sun somewhere hanging there
as a bulb in need of replacement.

The Fox Was Chased

from the bookstore with a broom
for reading Irish poetry and not replacing
books on the shelves in the right order.
His not-so-royal-anymore tail dropped
between his legs. He'd have bitten
the woman with the severe hang-up
against animals frequenting a bookstore,
but the broom with its angry teeth
scraped across his less-than-furry back.
Living in the forest was a hard life.
He risked his life crossing the road
to the beach each time and running
doglike down the city bicycle path.
He often wanted poetry to read,
while he wandered the beaches
and posed for cameras, ears
piqued to every spoken word.
Foxes never carried money
and were said not to read, but women
were animals just as foxes and wolves;
and he preferred Seamus Heaney.
He snuck into the bookstore when
no one was looking, and with his mouth
biting into the spine of a paperback,
he flung it down to the floor. There
he marveled at the sense of loneliness,
cold, and distant bright lights
visible down the street in snow—
even the taste of paper used
to print poetry. He knew winter,
and it knew him to be a pitiful beast.
He was a refined animal in spite
of a customer, turning to see a fox
with his mouth sunk in poetry,
shouting an alarm. And then the heavy-
shouldered woman, in spectacles
like headlights veering off a highway,
brought out the broom. Out of spite,
he lifted a royal leg to piss on the carpet,
just to show them poetry was real.

On a Bus Headed the Wrong Way in Watts

Not good at anything, he had written down
        the wrong address, and as a stranger in LA,
he recognized the only white man on the bus
           was him, as the old woman clucked her tongue
at his color and brought up gospel from her chest.
        A freight train cried lord almighty with its empty
boxcars. Turning around from his seat, a stage
          from which to sing out, "You know she's waiting,
just anticipating," the bus driver worried over
        this boy now, in a falsetto deepening, knew
he had to try a little tenderness, and asked
          if he had any friends where he was going.

Behind the wheel he named streets no longer there.
        A white-haired man sang, "Ain't here none of them,"
as he edged forward on his seat. The bus driver
          repeated what he said to the white boy, who
was on his soul quest. He was only eighteen,
        in a tweed jacket he had slipped on
before running away from home. Now each block
          brought him closer to the understanding
he must get off, head back, find another way.
        He wore glasses too large for his face, bangs that never
obeyed a comb, his world being a refrigerator where
          every thought mildewed.

The freight train in its frantic cry rose above
        the nightmare billboards. The soul driver
shook his head. "I know you got no one,"
          his voice this engine revving its gears
on beat-up blacktop. "Better run when you get off the next stop."
        The boy waved his hand through his refractory hair,
stood up from his seat. "Lord, let him be spared,"
          said the old woman with her one white eye riding
above her eyelashes. And the boy ran best
        he could past the others he imagined
wanting his jacket; "tweed," they would scream,
          wanting their fingers on it.

Richard Brautigan Wants to Walk Off the Cover of *Trout Fishing in America*

He's standing by Ben Franklin's statue
and thinking Ben would like to walk away, too,
out of all this marble. What has trout fishing
to do with the American Revolution, and Brautigan,
whose pilgrim hippie hat tops his cool San Francisco
look in Washington Square, keeps his hands
behind his back. His big wire-rimmed stare
at the photographer confirms everything
he's thinking. The slick black boots of his lady
want to walk away from this stone furniture,
unaware of Ben Franklin's thoughts, maybe the same
as Brautigan's of rivers running thick with trout.
Or snow that falls on the land, in some places
with frozen bunkers where hunters gather
to murder deer. I read the book in high school,
wanting to unlace the boots of the lady,
wondering if I could ever talk with her rationally.
Or be older than nineteen. I never cared about
catching fish, only words, and years later,
not so many really, I met Brautigan, checked him
in to the far northern hotel where he'd sleep
after his reading. I went up there to adjust his leaky toilet.
On his hotel bed he had a fifth of vodka
and a *Playboy*; he wasn't going to take any chances
for a good time. I never wonder what Hemingway's
up to, nor cared that he breathed in a shotgun
one night because the words weren't falling
from tumor to typewriter on a desk in Idaho.
A desk clerk did his job, but nothing was leaking
except all of this that took forty years to shape.

Dream House

If I ever slept here I don't remember.
Let me say I have dreamed in this space, though,
and on a cold January morning, my dream self
wakes up in another bed, not winter
in this rather small house, with the front window open
to the smell of apples. Perhaps I have added
apples to remember a kind of roundness
to a woman, who could be there or not.
Whatever I do feels wrong somehow, intruding
somewhere I don't live and the woman,
whose eyebrows are nests, accepts my presence
as temporary, always moving out but not gone,
for who would watch her daughter.
The floor is covered with the debris
of living too fast for having so little, socks
with their tunnel that feet are driven through
early in the morning and the queen of hearts
turns up from this greasy deck of cards.
What address this house is can't be determined.
Sometimes it's far away and the idea
of moving is troublesome. But I rise
to my feet, and regard her daughter,
who has wandered out to the yard.
A quiet day of birds has begun, and her mother
resists any urge to be a bird herself, lifted off
in flight, but lies on the bed now,
her rump of sandstone raised up or eyes full
of water drunk in prisons, until I wake up
in my own bed, serenaded by snowplows,
their blades low down and scraping.

At the Los Angeles Central Library

In the 811 section, in my desert hat still,
the same black shoes that wandered down the Mojave Road
one sunset, I thought I'd last forever.
Three of my books were on the shelf. But I was alone.
My son had dropped me off, like a father
delivering his son to the library for his education.
Ray Bradbury visited another California library
every day and found his career in books.
He wrote *Fahrenheit 451* on a basement typewriter,
fed nickels in to type and spent approximately
nine dollars on a classic. I wasn't Bradbury,
nickel-fed typewriters had disappeared like phone booths
and, well, like typewriters themselves. I had come to read.
Maybe sit at one of the long tables with reading lamps,
and write. The Mojave taught me to keep my eyes
to the ground, for the rattle coils of snakes, footpaths
of ghosts, volcanic rock on desert road, holes
rodents dug down to escape the day; taught me
to look at the light, in its blizzard of heat, to find
laughter in anger—my body on fire, it seemed—
to watch a poem float by. Happy to be there in history,
inside these books, a stranger from the desert,
in his sun hat, shoes with sand in them,
the same khaki-colored shirt I'd worn for days.
Happy to have walked down to the nearest
7-Eleven store to buy a candy bar from a man
wearing a turban. At that corner, one could vanish
into a neighborhood and never return, live in a box,
saving up change for a hamburger. Every day hunger
would be a mountain, a prehistoric lake bed
to cross. In the library, I thought about
that eighteen-year-old boy who had hitchhiked
to California, in the October that Janis Joplin
died—who now stood before his own books,
and waited for his cell phone to ring, his son to say
he was outside; and I would leave behind
the evidence that I once lived upon earth.

Three poetry books and the fourth I left
with the lady at the information desk
for somebody named Murphy in acquisitions,
whom I had spoken with briefly downstairs.
I thought I'd last as long as the Mojave Road,
over a hundred years, a stranger in the city, and had survived
112 degrees at noon, my shadow breaking
under my feet, but LA now felt like home.

Electric Morning

Bush Street, Downtown San Francisco

Sunday morning stepping through
a dirt-encrusted alley, we carry our old dreams
to the practice room. Good friends, we play
with fire, we could strike those matches
against misery here, but we no longer smoke—and
haul guitars and keyboard past the homeless
with their heads all awhirl on Bush Street.

Sunday is a moan for the tears gone
dry after four young men died
in a stolen car around the corner; but we come
armed to play, coffee fueling that aplomb
a little longer while a girl's pink ukulele's
stroked happily in the nervous breakdown
of someone who'll smoke in the key of high
where we parked our Lexus in the alley—
stop and look around, who's to blame
for any of this, not us, going back to the ceiling wax
where we'll play till our fingers melt,
in the basement of the old hotel.

Downtown there's a kind of quiet
that matches us walking to our gig;
it's not all over now despite being sixty;
perhaps it's the soiled sidewalk,
balled-up dreams tossed every which way,
an aroma of coffee dark as unwashed windows;
listen closely, "Ruby Tuesday" spins
on an old stereo-record changer
in my sixteen-year-old head, the songs
we will practice tidied up with chords
whose strides take us around the corner
to plug into the amplifier and be loud—
anything else than who we are.

Montgomery Clift Talks in That Slow, Rounded Way of Someone Desperately Drunk

Marilyn Monroe caresses the ailing rodeo rider
      who leans against her polka dots
outside the Dayton Bar in Nevada, those polka dots
          all over her dress, like mumps, and the car door
open where they both share the same close-up.
      The misfits broken up inside and out,
Montgomery no longer the pretty boy—

his scars covered by makeup—and the camera like a thief
      stealing from beauty, showing his cheekbones
sculpted hard as hubcaps after his accident
          on Tower Road coming down that steep hill
from Liz Taylor's party while they were shooting *Raintree County.*
      All that Hollywood in him gone: broken teeth pulled
out of his choking throat, his '55 Chev's face smashed—

in every gesture now something's damaged, and Marilyn Monroe,
      that mother, aging more each frame of film
and avoiding the camera, as if her own face would cave
          from the impact of feeling.
In John Huston's movie, death always speaks between silences.
      Let the cameras run, he says.
Perce Howland, a cowboy forbidden to return to his ranch

since his mother remarried. His life buried in gauze with all
      those family secrets that he claws at—
the earth mother in her white hair not blonde
          or any earthly color but a lie. She finds the screeching crash
      again in his forehead in the longest
Hollywood suicide. Her dress skintight for the next
      cue through each busty breath
          swimming under the hot lights,
in the last movie she'll ever make.

Selective Service Decision to Defer Him after His Psychiatrist Wrote a Letter

He couldn't kill anyone but himself,
and even that he couldn't do.
He lay in the hospital bed after
his suicide, and heard someone dying
several beds away. Her screams
from a darkness no one wanted
to hear, for she was afraid to die.
He remembered the body bags
televised on the tarmac about
to be flown back from Vietnam.
His doctor was named Slaughter,
who asked him questions of his love life.
He didn't know what to say
after she checked his vitals
and suggested the psych unit upstairs.
There he lay without knowing
why he suffered so, knew boys
who had never made it home.
Boys who had triggered landmines
in Vietnam, and he shivered,
wondering if he had sacrificed
anything in his attempt to die
and grasped both his balls
to see if he still had them.

When Lake Superior Remembers the North Sea

A weight in the rain can be felt upon our shoulders
in open notebooks, as we try to write about what
matters: the ore boat with its noisy presence,
with rail cars unloading iron ore; the rain falling
through the leaves in their softly growing chants
of anger; the whitecaps that don't say who drowned
today or years ago, in their melancholy wash.
The waves, like so many Viking prows, push
against the breakwall, wanting landfall before
we can say more. And I imagine on this stormy
day bearded men whose eyes stare out at
the vastness of water where nothing
survives for long. Maybe I am one of them, too.
We are brothers in middle age, and sucking a deep breath
in the rain, I remember love like a pole axe
driven through metal or wood. How it hurt
and often destroyed. Never relented
but struck deep before it was withdrawn.
And I say nothing about her to my friend
who sits at the picnic table with me, here
to witness carnage, but she had long brown hair,
sunburned eyelids when she stood beside me naked.
In a lonely room, just bed and table, some
vinyl for the phonograph with scratchy needle.
Like Mimi Farina's record with her song
for Janis Joplin played over and over
in the quiet of the morning. In a room
with a view of the harbor and its ore dock.
I see her in dreams waiting for me to come
downstairs. She and her daughter
at the kitchen table, and when I touch her
the dream vanishes. And I ache. That pole
axe going deep. A steady drizzle has become deluge.
The notebook's damp, so many words
a smudge of something no longer there.
With our caps sunk low over straining brows,
we let our fingers fidget cold at the picnic table—
poets in the rain, whose words turn darker
than they should, in that whorl so tightly
wrung we have to rise and walk away.

When I Was a Night Clerk Living with My Girlfriend at the Hotel

I was late for work so many times
         the desk clerks laughed
when I showed up, knowing I lived
         in a room on the fifth floor
with my nineteen-year-old girlfriend, Emily.
               We should all have a girlfriend
named Emily, in a one-room home
         with a hot plate

where spaghetti was always dinner.
         (If not spaghetti, then chili night
downstairs in the pub, nights of popcorn
         beforehand.) A girlfriend who didn't
              mind that the worn white sheets
were changed once a month by housekeeping if we
         switched rooms.

I was always late, counting down the seconds
         of timelessness that existed there,
where characters from the Great American Novel
         never left the hotel, like the hotel guest,
             a neurotic in polyester, who called
to tell me his phone was on fire.
         He wasn't to be believed, but then the operator rang.

The hotel was always on the edge of burning.
         Abbott and Costello slept here once,
but I checked in Brautigan and writers
         who deserved nothing but a six o'clock
             wake-up call for treating women
the way they did after readings. I sent Emily
         to investigate for smoke, though

she wasn't on staff; and there a burnt phone
         smoldered in a maniac's room,
plastic melted down to bad karma
         paraded downstairs by the manager.
             Maybe Hemingway would have made
Emily into a femme fatale of nineteen,
         or John Voelker in his best district attorney

voice would have put her into a fishing
                boat and let her drift in the moonlight.
A nineteen-year-old killer, no, my black-haired
                girl kept Ernest away from our door.
                                I was a workingman behind the desk.
The rooms mostly vacant, a switchboard
                to connect incoming calls, nobody paying

their rent but the weekenders out for a good time.
                I saw the best minds forget who they were
and where they lived, spin the revolving door
                into the blizzard, for a taste of the night,
                                the fireworks of a lowered blade
that caught the icy road just right. And the end
                for many came every Monday when

the money was due, and renters
                had to pay up or leave. And we kept on
because I convinced the desk clerks
                they needed to hire me for their nights off,
                                and all of them left me there to answer
the switchboard, count out the till,
                while upstairs in a small room Emily

chilled our milk on the ledge of the window.
                Everyone should have the chance
to be in love with a girl named Emily, watch the stars
                from the fifth-floor fire escape,
                                and when no one is looking
match the fireworks in the snowplow
                with each kiss.

Your Table Peopled with Characters

Lord, forgive me my dizzy headlights;
small towns in Minnesota overwhelm me
alone at this coffee shop table.

Henry Zender tips his bowler
to a fat moon and remembers yellow parasols
of women from Alsace-Lorraine.

He's drunk. And Private Reese has veered out of this poem
and strides toward Belle Isle, after garroting
a German boy with a broken wine bottle

hid like a gun under his coat in an abandoned
church. But no church is ever alone,
for there's heartache in the Lord's face—

sometimes a midnight grin
when he knows the fate of Henry at Belle Isle,
Reese in Hitler's bathtub in Munich.

His flashbulb shot the naked *Vogue*
photographer, Lee Miller, first
before he climbed in with her wearing his helmet.

Somewhere those flatbeds want to close the gap
between heartache and love. I sip coffee.
Winter serves me, our favorite character,

and I want to run away with her,
because she's so thin and loveable,
any words spoken are erasable,

but I search for them inside me.
And I know this matters to you, it always
does, your table is peopled with characters

you can't control. Winter watches me,
her coffee dark as the road somewhere else;
she lets me drink coffee for free.

I've never understood the difference
between dreams and waking, or driving miles
without ever returning home.

But I ache for the poem not written,
so do you, who vanishes in words
on a snowy highway headed nowhere.

A road taken without leaving your chair,
except you have miles to go,
praying for that miracle.

When it happens you understand
your fingers' disorder
running across the page

trying to catch a ghost of a word
barely whispered, the moon
in its candlelight burning inside.

Acknowledgments

The author wishes to acknowl-
edge the following publishers of the
poems included in this volume: *Bop Dead
City*: "The Mountains Didn't Know I Was
Playing a Piano"; *Pirene's Fountain, Silk and Spice
Issue*: "Billy the Kid Smells Cinnamon in Texas after
a Bad Night"; *Prairie Schooner*: "Reese's Letter to a Son,"
"Gravitational Field," and "Scars"; *Slab*: "Walt Whitman Wears
a Huge Hat in the Noonday Heat" and "On a Bus Headed East on
US 2 in a Late-Night Blizzard Years Ago"; *Queen City Music Anthology*,
with Mike Waite on guitar: "Across the Street from His House, a Boy,
the Oldest of Sixteen, at His Father's Grave"; *Slant:* "Union Soldier,
after Abandoning His Battle, Forgets Everything Wading through the
Shallows"; and *Solstice:* "Montgomery Clift Talks in That Slow, Rounded
Way of Someone Desperately Drunk" and "Selective Service Decision to
Defer Him after His Psychiatrist Wrote a Letter."

A poem read on Michigan Radio while poet laureate of the Upper Pen-
insula: *"When One Tugs at a Single Thing in Nature, He Finds It Attached
to the Rest of the World."* And on WNMU FM in Marquette: "Union Sol-
dier, after Abandoning His Battle, Forgets Everything Wading through
the Shallows," "The Butcher," and "Dream House." But the following
poems were recorded with electric guitar accompaniment by Radio
On for a CD entitled *Electric Landscapes*: "Sergeant Reese Loves to Box
Away His Pain," "Billy the Kid Smells Cinnamon in Texas after a Bad
Night," "Union Soldier, after Abandoning His Battle, Forgets Every-
thing Wading through the Shallows," and *"Love Allows Us to Walk in the
Sweet Music of Our Particular Heart."*

Thanks to: Peter Markus and Jonathan Johnson for reading everything,
and Rodney Torreson, who saw many poems in their raw states; the
bandmates of Radio On, Jeremy Morelock, Dylan Trost, Ian Crane,
Thane Padilla, and Claudia Drosen; my old Birmingham garage mates,
Chris Robinson and John Lewandowski; and my California poet
friends, Susan Kelly-DeWitt, Stephen Linsteadt, and
Maria Elena B. Mahler.

More thanks to the Peter White Public Library staff, in Marquette, for letting me work hours on end there.

This thankfulness without words to Annie Martin.

Notes

Somewhere We'll Leave the World is taken from one of my favorite Philip Levine collections, *The Names of the Lost*, and the poem "A Late Answer."

"Scars" happened on Woodward Avenue in a friend's Volkswagen, after coming back from the Selective Service office in Pontiac.

The Reese poems, of father, son, and grandfather, come from watching *Hell Is for Heroes*, an American war film of 1962, and the character played by Steve McQueen, Pvt. John Reese.

The garage band poems take place in Birmingham, Michigan, where I grew up across from Holy Name Church, and the bandmates are Chris Robinson and John Lewandowski.

"Lately My Resemblance to Captain Beefheart Has Been Disturbing" is a completely true Detroit story.

"Detroit, on the Bus Headed Downtown, the Driver Is Listening to Chopin's Preludes" refers to a dream of riding the bus down Woodward and the Philip Levine poem "An Abandoned Factory, Detroit."

"Without Work" uses a number of lines from a Henry Miller essay in *Black Spring:* "The Angel Is My Watermark."

"Love Allows Us to Walk in the Sweet Music of Our Particular Heart" is taken from a Jack Gilbert poem, "The Great Fires," and is the very last line of the poem—and several lines from that poem are referenced in another poem, "Hollywood."

The poems "John Huston Talks to Clark Gable about His Next Scene as a Drunk Falling Off a Car Hood" and "Montgomery Clift Talks in That Slow, Rounded Way of Someone Desperately Drunk" come from watching *The Misfits,* an American drama written by Arthur Miller and directed by John Huston.

"The Blind Guitarist Whose Six Strings Can Only Play Him So Far" refers to a character of the same name from my noir set in Mexico, *Salt and Blood.*

"Walt Whitman Wears a Huge Hat in the Noonday Heat" comes from an artist's residency in the Mojave National Preserve.

Russell Thorburn is the author of *Father, Tell Me I Have Not Aged* (Marick Press, 2006). A National Endowment for the Arts recipient and first poet laureate of the Upper Peninsula, he lives in Marquette with his wife. His poems have appeared in many literary journals and anthologies, including *Prairie Schooner, Sou'wester, Quarterly West,* and *Third Coast.*